About the Author

Norman Marks, CPA, CRMA is an evangelist for "better run business", focusing on corporate governance, risk management, internal audit, enterprise performance, and the value of information. He is also a mentor to individuals and organizations around the world.

Norman was the chief audit executive of major global corporations for twenty years and is a globally-recognized thought leader in the professions of internal auditing and risk management. In addition, he has served as chief risk officer, compliance officer, and ethics officer, and managed what would now be called the IT governance function (information security, contingency planning, methodologies, standards, etc.) He ran the Sarbanes-Oxley Section 404 (SOX) programs and investigation units at several companies.

He is the author of the Institute of Internal Auditors' "Management's Guide to Sarbanes-Oxley Section 404: Maximize Value Within Your Organization"), which has been described as "the best Sarbanes-Oxley 404 guide out there for management".

Norman is a member of the review boards of several audit and risk management publications (including the magazines of ISACA and the IIA), a frequent speaker internationally, the author of multiple award-winning articles, and a prolific blogger about better run business (consistently rating as one of the top global influencers in social media on the topics of GRC, internal audit, risk management, and governance).

Norman was profiled in publications of the AICPA and the IIA as an innovative and successful internal auditing leader. He has also been honored as a Fellow of the Open Compliance and Ethics Group for his GRC thought leadership, and as an Honorary Fellow of the Institute of Risk Management for his contributions to risk management.

Contents

2

Introduction

Consultants and other thought leaders (including software vendors) are pressing boards and executives to ensure their organizations have effective governance, risk management, and compliance (GRC).

Many of the consultants have built practices around GRC. For example, Deloitte, KPMG, and PwC all offer Governance, Risk, and Compliance consulting services (EY offers consulting services for GRC technology).

What should board directors, executive management, and those who advise them (including risk and audit practitioners) know about GRC? Is it really the imperative that is suggested by the various white papers?

What is "GRC"? Is it more than a single collective bucket into which the firms have gathered all their consulting services for governance?

In this discussion, I suggest 12 questions that you may ask about GRC, whether to understand the term or to assess its adequacy. I will then review additional considerations for organizations considering technology to upgrade their "GRC" processes.

I put "GRC" in quotes because there is no common understanding of what the expression "governance, risk management, and compliance" really means. I joke that GRC really means "governance, risk management, and **confusion**" because there are so many interpretations.

So before getting to my list of 12 questions *about* GRC, we need to answer the burning question of what GRC means.

The GRC Mystery

Some use the term to refer to the efficient integration of compliance programs and risk management across the enterprise. It is true that this is a serious issue for many organizations: when compliance is fragmented (i.e., independent functions address individual compliance requirements without coordination), it is both inefficient and likely to fail; when risk management is fragmented (the typical organization of size has at least seven independent functions addressing different areas of risk without coordination) it is impossible to understand the inter-relationship of risks and have a reliable view of risk across the enterprise; and, while many practitioners believe they should be separated, there is a natural relationship between risk management and compliance – after all, the failure to meet compliance obligations is a risk that needs to be managed. To see which consultants use GRC to mean "risk and compliance", take one of their white papers and substitute the phrase "risk and compliance" whenever they say "GRC" and see whether that makes the text clearer.

Others mean risk management when they say GRC. They may be referring to the problem of fragmented risk management, as mentioned earlier. Unfortunately, some consultants are using the term "GRC" as if it is a synonym for risk management – which it is not.

Again, the way to see if this is what they mean is to replace "GRC" with "risk management" in their papers. Why do they say "GRC" when they mean "risk management"? I suspect it's a combination of ignorance (they don't understand the importance of referring to governance, of the need described below to consider how various aspects of the organization work in harmony) and seizing the opportunity to use the latest buzzword to create hype and buzz about their services.

Many refer to a select set of functions and processes, influenced by software analysts like Forrester and Gartner who rate software using categories (of which GRC is one) and the software vendors who market GRC solutions. To them, GRC generally means risk management, compliance management, policy management, and internal audit management – integrated so that they use common risk registers, etc. While this is an interesting combination for software vendors, it is not, in my experience and opinion, representative of the priorities and business challenges facing organizations. For example, many organizations do not change their policies very often and optimizing policy management is not a priority for them. So, I don't recommend that this be the interpretation of GRC used to understand and assess potential issues within an organization. (By the way, there are other code names for combinations of software such as "GRC platform", "Enterprise GRC", and so on. My view is that this just adds to the GRC confusion without helping address business challenges.)

You may note that the definitions of GRC above make little, if any, reference to "governance" processes. Yet:

1. Many of the failures of organizations over the last years have been attributed to failures in governance and risk management. Even compliance failures (such as BP's Gulf disaster and the Barclays Bank LIBOR issue) have been blamed, at least in part, on poor governance.

2. Risk management is about the achievement of strategies and objectives, which are established and performance against which is managed in governance processes.

3. Governance processes ensure that risk management and compliance programs are effective and meet the needs of the organization.

I ascribe to and advocate a definition of GRC that, in my opinion, makes business sense. It adds value by helping understand the real-life problems that can inhibit the delivery of optimized value by an organization. It discusses risk management and compliance within the *context* of governance, and when it talks about GRC it is talking about *all* the processes within an organization that have to function effectively to ensure optimized, sustainable, agile, long-term, compliant, and responsible performance.

The definition I advocate is from the Open Compliance and Ethics Group[iii] (OCEG):

> "GRC is a capability that enables an organization to reliably achieve objectives while addressing uncertainty and acting with integrity "

This includes effective board operations, performance management, and other aspects of organizational governance together with risk management, compliance, and internal audit – with the shared objective of delivering sustained, ethical, optimized value to the stakeholders.

GRC refers, in OCEG's and my view, to the integrated and orchestrated operation of the various functions required to deliver value to stakeholders. While it is important for the parts to work well individually, it is essential that they work *together*. For example, if objectives and strategies are set without an understanding of related risks, they may not be the optimal strategies for the organization and, furthermore, are unlikely to be achieved. If risk officers do not understand and address risks to the overall objectives of the organization, it is highly unlikely that they are considering the more significant risks to the delivery of value. If corporate strategies and objectives are not understood by every manager, how can the organization expect those managers to make decisions to further those objectives? In addition, if you optimize each function and process individually with the 'perfect' application systems for each, you will create a hodgepodge of different technologies that is near impossible to manage, expensive to operate, a headache when it comes to security, and anything but agile.

So, effective GRC means that the organization is working in harmony to achieve shared objectives in addition to each function being separately efficient and effective.

Questions to ask about GRC

It is now time to turn to the questions that board members and executives can ask to assess whether their organization has effective GRC. This is not a comprehensive list and each organization may see fit to add to or change it as appropriate. The questions are also intended to start a discussion of each point; in other words, an executive can ask one of these questions and then ask additional, more probing questions depending on the answer received.

1. Are goals and strategies to achieve them clearly established and communicated across the organization, so that there are common goals and objectives?

While it is routine for a board to work with management and approve the organization's goals, objectives, and strategies, many do not ensure that they are clearly communicated to everybody whose actions should be harnessed to those goals and objectives. Instead, individual or group goals (and therefore compensation targets) are based upon local objectives that may be inconsistent with or irrelevant to the achievement of organizational goals.

Even when there is an apparent linkage to organizational goals, the latter are often expressed at a high level without detailing who needs to do what and what assumptions have been made. As a result, individual managers interpret the organizational goals in their own way – and put corporate achievement at risk.

Let me illustrate with an example. At one of my former companies, all the managers were provided a list of the corporate objectives. We were asked to define our objectives with these in mind and indicate which corporate objective each of our personal objectives supported. While it is true to say that our individual objectives and performance measurement were linked to corporate objectives, it is highly likely that we were not doing everything required from us if the organization was to achieve the corporate objectives. A better process would have taken each of the corporate objectives, identified what needed to be done by whom to achieve them, and then assigned those to the appropriate individuals as their personal objectives.

In addition, achieving some goals may require compromise with others. Take the example of a company that has goals of increasing both revenue and operating margins, with strategies that include managing personnel cost. One arm of the organization is planning a move into a new geography, requiring additional local sales and support personnel, but the human resources (HR) function has set spending (budget) targets that do not permit the addition of a recruitment specialist for the area. As a result, the new initiative stumbles. While HR achieves its local goals, it fails to support achievement of the corporate revenue goal.

Another example might be an organization that has goals of enhancing customer satisfaction and moving products to the cloud. The product development team decides that the only new development will be 'in the cloud', but existing customers using 'on premise' solutions are clamoring for additional functionality and are not ready to move to the cloud. Unless somebody on the executive floor takes control, achievement of one goal (cloud product development) may be at the expense of another (customer satisfaction) where the organization cannot afford to fail.

Many organizations keep their organizational objectives and goals secret from the general employee population. The concern is that competitors and others (such as potential customers and vendors) might leverage that information for advantage. But, when managers making operational and even strategic decisions are unaware of the strategies and objectives set by the executive management team and approved by the board, is it likely that they will always act as desired?

As with many problems, including those in this publication, correction of this problem requires leadership from the top, a recognition that it not only exists but impedes success, and the assignment of corrective actions to senior managers.

2. Does the organization work in harmony, sharing information and working towards shared goals?

Do the culture, systems, processes, and structure of the organization provide both the will and the capacity to move the organization in the same direction?

- Do the board and executives work as a team or are individual members competing for position and power? This question can be extended into groups and project teams as well.

- Is there sufficient sharing of individual and group objectives so each executive (and manager) can help the other?

- Do the different areas of the business communicate with each other, or are they in isolated offices and virtual silos and keep information to themselves as a source of power?

- Are the executives rewarded for team or individual performance? What will drive actions if there's a conflict?

- Does the employee performance recognition and appraisal process encourage or discourage teamwork? For example, do employees compete for a top rating, potentially sabotaging each other?

- Is there a single 'source of truth' or do different organizations maintain different numbers (e.g., for revenue pipeline)?

- Is risk information shared, so each area can see how risks inter-relate and how they impact each other?

- When it comes to the allocation of resources (budget, people), is it based on 'community' priorities? Are departments willing to share their resources when needed by another?

For some, knowledge is power. The more valuable employee is the one that shares their knowledge, helps others when they have a need, and makes other people's priorities their own.

I believe most organizations suffer from this cultural malady. Executive actions is needed to change the culture and reset expectations – and reward people for actions that benefit the many rather than the few.

3. Is there integration between strategy-setting and risk, performance management and risk, budget and strategy, strategy and compliance, etc.?

To be effective, many functions, processes, and activities need to be closely integrated. That doesn't necessarily mean the systems have to be integrated, just the operation of those activities. For example:

- When objectives and strategies are set by management and approved by the board, is sufficient risk information available and are those with insights into the risks involved? For example, does management know what the levels of risk are when it chooses among strategy options or sets target achievement levels? Do they realize they are choosing between strategy A (which has a 80% chance of delivering at least $8m in additional revenue, a 10% likelihood of reaching $10m, but a 20% probability of failing to hit the target of $8m), and strategy B (which is 90% likely to get to $8m or more, 2% likely to reach $10m or more, and only 10% likely to miss the $8m target). Do they include as part of their decision actions to modify those risks and increase the likelihood of success?

- When risks change, or new risks emerge, are those responsible for strategy informed promptly so that objectives and strategies can be modified if necessary?

- Does management monitor performance based only on results and projections, or is risk information included? Is management happy to see the business running at 100 mph, but not watching to see whether there is a wall 100 feet away? How confident is management in the forecast – and what can or should be done to address the uncertainty involved? For example, if there is only an 80% confidence level in the revenue projection, what are the downside risks (and what can be done to minimize them) and the upside opportunities (and what can be done to realize them)?

- When cash flow becomes tight, or earnings projected to fall short, are strategies revisited? I have seen major projects continued despite such warnings and then shut down far too quickly when managers realize they no longer have the cash to complete the project.

- Similarly, when cash becomes scarce, is this considered in the risk management process?

- Does the compliance function participate in strategy decisions? Are the implications and risks related to compliance considered when deciding when and how to enter a new market? Or does the compliance function have to 'chase the bus' to address requirements after the decision has been made – introducing additional cost and risk?

- Do risk and compliance professionals share information? After all, the risk of non-compliance (and its related effect on the organization's reputation) is often one of the more significant risk areas for the enterprise.

- Do internal audit, risk management, and compliance share information? Do they separate, independent and siloed assessments of risk?

When different parts of the organization work in silos, even if those silos run with beautiful efficiency and precision, the whole may be ineffective.

Sometimes, managers must make compromises in their own areas for the collective good, but that requires collaboration and a desire to work together without fear of being held to account when your individual area or personal goals are less than perfect.

Organizations need to acknowledge that failures to collaborate significantly impede success. In fact, organizations tend to succeed in spite of their failure to work together. The executive management team needs to set a new tone and take actions where the failure to collaborate is worst.

4. Are functions/processes/systems fragmented, inhibiting performance?

One of the original drivers of "GRC" was the fact that most companies have multiple functions for risk management (the typical organization of size has seven just for risk management) and compliance. These diverse groups are not coordinated, let alone integrated, with the result that some aspects of risk and compliance are covered by multiple groups (increasing cost) and other areas fall in between the gaps.

When multiple groups assess and manage risk in silos (such as just looking at IT-related risk, or only risk related to sourcing of key components), it is nearly impossible to gain a view of risk for the enterprise as a whole. Often, these groups use different language, different standards, different processes and systems, and report to management in different ways. They may even have significantly different assessments of the same risk. Not only is this inefficient, but the inter-relationship of risk is generally missed (such as how a failure in an IT process could impact recruiting, or supply chain affect an IT project), and management and the board may lack the risk information it needs to run the business.

Fragmentation in compliance is also very common. For example, I worked at a global manufacturing company that had five factories in China. Each had to comply with China's export regulations, but instead of cooperating they handled the task independently. Rather than sharing a full-time expert in the regulations, they each made it a part-time task of an employee in the accounting function (with minimal training) and purchased different systems for the mandated reporting. As a direct result, all but one were soon out of compliance.

For another (similar) view of the problem of fragmentation, I recommend a piece by Michael Rasmussen on "Inevitability of Failure: Managing GRC in Silos" (at http://www.grc2020.com/).

The problem of fragmentation is not limited to the risk management and compliance functions. It can be a problem in other disciplines (such as credit management, and I have also seen it in IT). But the more common and arguably more significant issue is when systems and related processes are fragmented.

How can a company's management make decisions in today's fast-moving environment without timely, reliable information? Yet, companies still have multiple ERP and other systems and rely on spreadsheets to give them consolidated views of the enterprise. How can that provide decision-makers on the executive floor the information they need to run the business with confidence? I doubt they realize either the risk they are running or the ability of today's technology to solve their problems.

A closely related problem occurs when multiple functions or groups have overlapping responsibilities. For example, information security at a division may be 'audited' or assessed by the internal audit group, the external auditor, the corporate information security function, an ISO auditor, and more. This is highly inefficient and disruptive to the operations of the audited area. The other side of the coin is that at the same time that there are overlaps and redundancies, there may also be gaps in coverage. When everybody only sees their assigned pieces of the jigsaw, it is quite possible for a piece to be missing and nobody notice because nobody sees the entire picture.

The way forward is to recognize that fragmentation is an issue and initiate a project to identify where it exists and the risk it represents. Then, owners can be assigned with responsibility for organization and/or systems changes to correct the situation.

5. Does the organization have a culture that embraces performance, intelligent taking of risk, and compliance with laws, regulations, and society's expectations?

Thought leaders have been writing about organizational culture for a long time. Many were interested in assuring organizational values, ethics, and integrity. Others focused on compliance, both with external laws and regulations and with internal standards and policies.

More recently, the discussion has turned to the notion of a "culture of greed".

The culture of every organization affects its behavior. For example:

- How aggressive or passive are managers and executives in driving employees and others (such as vendors and channel partners) to perform?
- Are they so aggressive that they are willing to take risks beyond levels acceptable to the organization?
- Are they so passive that opportunities fly by without being noticed? Is so much time taken deciding whether to take the risk that "time expires"?
- Is failure punished so severely that risks are not taken?
- Is failure too easily accepted, so more risks are taken than appropriate?
- Are they so busy performing that they fail even to consider compliance requirements?
- Does management listen to the compliance professionals? Do the risk officers have a voice?
- Are they willing to risk compliance issues in order to turn a profit?
- Is everybody advancing their own interests (compensation, power, etc.) over those of the organization? Is this an accepted behavior?

- Do units compete unhealthily? (I worked at a company where two of our factories bid on a major contract with a telecom company; they continued to lower their bids even when the field was reduced to two – and they were fully aware who the other bidder was.)
- Is the long-term sacrificed for short-term rewards?
- Do executives and the board trivialize societal expectations, or are they given prioritized over performance?
- Are employees valued? Really? Do they believe they are valued and perform accordingly?
- How great is the pressure on employees to perform? Is it too much, too little, or just right?

One interesting 'test' is to walk around the offices or factory floors and see what is posted. If you see group performance and safety metrics that are current and clearly part of discussions at group meetings, you are seeing signs of a healthy culture.

Another test is to see how many people leave, and how they leave, at 'quitting time'. When everybody stays and are clearly relieved to be heading home (or to the nearest watering hole), you might question their commitment to the firm. When many stay and appear totally stressed, you might worry about pressures may lead them to cut corners. But when people are happily chatting about the business and results, the culture is more likely to be healthy.

Culture can be excessively aggressive or passive. Striking and maintaining the right balance is not easy, but is essential to delivering sustained performance, considering risks, and remaining in compliance.

Leadership from the CEO and active support from the entire executive team is necessary to correct this issue.

6. Is performance measured and rewarded consistent with delivery of value, achievement of objectives, and organizational values – long and well as short-term?

This is a question about two related things: the monitoring and measurement of performance, and how (and if) management incents desired behavior and results.

In their 2009 report, "Corporate Governance and the Financial Crisis: Key Findings and Main Messages" (at www.oecd.org), the Organisation for Economic Co-Operation and Development (OECD) identified:

- A lack of independence in the setting of objectives and measurement of performance
- Weak relationships between performance and remuneration
- Complex compensation programs that made it difficult to relate remuneration to performance
- Performance was not measured using metrics defined when strategies and goals are established.
- Compensation was not always linked to long-term performance.
- Risk was not considered when evaluating performance.

One of the interesting comments was that "remuneration and incentive systems that should be the focus of board (and sometimes regulatory) oversight need to be considered broadly and not just focused on the chief executive officer and board members". I interpret this as recognizing that compensation drives performance across the entire organization, so focusing only on the top executives ignores the strong likelihood that the people making decisions in the front lines may be incented by bonus programs that are not consistent with organizational goals (see above).

For example, consider the age-old issue of "empty revenue". Many, if not the majority of companies set goals for sales and other employees based on revenue. This tends to encourage them to make decisions that grow revenue irrespective of the level of profit, customer satisfaction (e.g., knowingly selling products and services that don't quite meet customer needs), and long-term value (e.g., moving revenue into the current quarter at a lower profit margin than if the sale was made in the next quarter).

Some years ago, my company acquired a business where internal audit participated in the process of reviewing whether departments had met or exceeded their goals. During the transition, the head of the new subsidiary's audit team told me that he was denying the IT department's claim that it had fully satisfied the goal of delivering a new financial system by the end of the quarter. The denial was based on the fact that, while IT had technically achieved the objective of implementing the system (it was in production), not a single report had been written for the users. It reminded me of a similar situation when I was in public accounting and my client had signed a contract that specified delivery of a "general ledger system"; the vendor billed for completion under the contract even though they didn't provide a single report – not even a trial balance!

I would approach this question in a number of steps, a number of questions that help obtain an answer – and identify where there might be a gap:

a. Assuming that the strategies and goals for the organization are approved by the board and will deliver longer and shorter-term value, consistent with organizational values and in compliance with applicable laws and regulations, were appropriate metrics established to measure achievement of those strategies and goals?
b. How clear is the relationship between the metrics and compensation awards? Would a reasonable person agree that compensation is clearly linked to achievement of the strategies and goals, with an appropriate balance between shorter and longer-term performance?

c. If there are issues relative to risk-taking, or behavior consistent with organizational values, do they affect compensation awards?
d. Are the goals and strategies of each unit and manager clearly consistent with achievement of organizational goals? Is individual and unit performance measured based on their active contribution to the achievement of the goals, or are they motivated to behavior that is inconsistent with those goals and strategies?
e. Is performance against objectives and goals measured objectively and fairly?
f. Are performance awards consistent with stakeholder expectations for compensation?

A few years ago, my manager and I had an argument about his philosophy of rewarding employees based on results instead of recognizing the quality of performance. While he recognized that not only had I performed at or above his expectations, but that he didn't know of anybody who could have done more. However, the organization had not been able to leverage it to deliver revenue. His argument was that because my work had not met his revenue goals, my performance rating and bonus should be adversely affected.

My argument was that I had performed beyond his expectations and the failure of the organization to leverage it to drive new revenue was not within my control. I shared the example of two sales managers: the first lazed at home but, because his customers were expanding rapidly, he was able to deliver high levels of revenue; the second worked all hours and built trusted relationships with every member of his customers' management teams. But, his customers were in a region devastated by an economic downturn and were unable to buy the company's products – although they recognized, through the salesman's efforts, the value to their business. My manager would have given a major bonus to the first and none to the second. I told him that he should expect the first to leave the company.

The point is that compensation has not only to be based on performance but fair, recognizing quality performance even when business results may lag. Otherwise, quality employees who work hard but don't receive fair compensation for their efforts will leave and only the lazy will remain. Compensation strategy also has to take into account employee morale and the behavior (not just the results) that you want to drive across the organization. Over-compensating individuals (including the CEO) can be damaging to employee morale as well.

7. Does management (at all levels) have quality, reliable, timely, current, useful information readily available when and where they make decisions?

The quality of management decisions depends to a great degree on the quality of the information they receive. The better the information, the more likely they are to make the 'right' decision.

Consider these questions. All need to be addressed before we can conclude that management has the information they need to make quality decisions to deliver optimized performance that complies with all applicable laws and regulations.

a. **Is the information reliable?** How confident are you that the information is accurate? Does it come directly from the corporate systems, where it is secured and subject to internal controls, or is it 'massaged' in spreadsheets before it is given to the decision-maker? Are 'adjustments' made based on the decision-maker's or some analyst's judgment as part of the reporting process? If it is a report from a data warehouse, is that data store secure and can you be sure that the reports are working the way they should?

There are many stories of meetings where, for example, the CFO addresses a group of executives to discuss the period's results. When he shows a slide with the revenue pipeline by region, there is a chorus of dissent as the head of sales and the regional sales executives all say that the numbers are wrong – but each has a different number. I have seen situations where sales executives keep pipeline information on spreadsheets and don't enter them in the corporate systems immediately. I have also seen situations where an executive 'corrects' the numbers in the corporate system because he has "special insight".

b. **Is the information complete**, providing everything needed for a quality decision? For example, does it include not only performance but risk information? Do decision makers have the input from compliance personnel so they can assess the potential compliance requirements and risks? Do they have information from everybody that will be affected by the decision, as well as those whose actions are required to make the initiative a success?

For example, when considering a new venture that involves expanding into a new country, is the decision on whether and how to proceed fully informed? Is it based on input from Human Resources (about the availability of skilled personnel), Tax, Treasury (about cash management facilities and regulations), Compliance, Facilities and IT (about the ability to house and support the new country's personnel), and so on?

c. **Is the information current?** Is the information up-to-date, reflecting the current situation? Or is it based on financial statements that are weeks, if not months old? In some situations, information that is only an hour old may be out of date! The question becomes "is the information sufficiently current to make an informed decision?"

Some years ago, the CFO at my company told me he was tired of "managing through the rear view mirror". If he had a decision to make, he would ask his staff for the information he needed to base it on. But, none of the information was current. The company's operational data was only updated monthly in most cases, and financial information was not only monthly but not finalized for several days after the end of the month.

What his team did, which took time as well, was to take the last set of information in the corporate systems and then project what they believed to be activity since.

How old is the information managers use to make decisions? Is it too old to be valuable?

d. **Is the information timely?** Do managers get the information they need quickly, when they need to make a decision? The speed of business is accelerating; can managers afford to wait even hours to get the insight they need? Taking this one step further, sometimes the first set of information you receive only gives you a rough idea of the situation and you need to drill down into the data. How long does that take? Can you ask multiple questions and get the answers fast enough to make quality decisions?

Is there a risk that while your decision-makers are waiting for information you might lose a window of opportunity?

e. **Is the information useful?** When you have a business decision to make, you don't want a stack of reports. You want the answers, the information you need, clearly presented and easily understood. Do your decision-makers have that, or do they need to pore through the reports and try to find the information they need? Do they then have to run additional reports or call other people because the information is not clear, or even raises more questions than it answers?

It's an old expression, but it's still true: there is a huge difference between data and information. What do you have at your company?

f. **Is the information where the decision-makers are?** If an executive is traveling and trying to run the business from an airport lounge, is the information there – with her? Or is it with her assistant in the home office, who is trying to read it to her? Wouldn't you rather they see it themselves?

Not only do we have a global business world that is spinning faster, but executives and managers are global travelers that need to make fast decisions from all kinds of places. Can you afford for them not to have access to the information they need, when they need it, where they need it? The good news is that with the advances that have been made in mobile technology, this is now a solvable problem.

8. Is there a reliable view of risk across the organization?

This question speaks to the adequacy of risk management. For example:

- Is risk managed in silos or as an enterprise-wide program? For example, are there separate and independent functions to manage IT-related risk, currency risk, supply chain risk, investment risk, customer credit risk, etc.?
- Is risk reported in a consistent fashion based on its potential impact on organizational objectives? For example, is the risk of an IT-related issue measured in terms of 'IT threats' or the potential effect on revenue generation, collections, etc.?
- Do risk reports reflect current information, or is risk only managed every quarter – in other words, is the risk information current?
- Are all risks of significance to the decisions that have to be made monitored, measured, and managed?
- Are the right people involved in identifying, assessing, evaluating, and responding to risks? Are they the people responsible for performance in the area of the risk? Are they the best positioned to understand and respond?
- Does risk information flow to everybody who needs it?
- Is the risk management program effective and does it meet the needs of the organization (for example, has there been an internal audit of the risk management framework and process)?

As noted earlier, the consideration of risk has to be part of every decision across the organization. Too many consider risk management effective when all that is being done is a periodic review of a limited set of so-called "top risks", based on a point-in-time report that is probably already out of date.

Risk management has to be dynamic, iterative, and responsive to change (one of the objectives of risk management according to the ISO 3100:2009 global risk management standard).

The management of risk has to be owned by every manager within the organization, part of how they run the business every day.

9. Is the voice of risk heard?

Some of the failures of governance and risk management have occurred when those responsible for understanding the aggregate level of risk for the organization as a whole (whether in a risk office or in management) have not been heard. More senior management has either overridden or suppressed their views; in some cases, risk officers who have spoken up have been terminated.

The essence of this point is to ensure that those responsible for governing and managing the organization receive reliable risk information. If management filters risk information inappropriately, the impact on the quality of decisions can be significant.

The voice of risk needs to be heard both by top management and by the board. Each organization will need to determine how best to achieve this. For example, should the Chief Risk Officer report at a level within the organization that effectively guarantees he will be heard? What ability does the risk officer have to discuss risk with the board – and how appropriate is that? Care has to be taken to ensure that management retains responsibility for managing risk, and that can be damaged if a Chief Risk Officer is seen as being accountable for risk management.

This issue is not limited to those who have the title "risk officer". It also applies to individuals in other functions, such as Information Security, Health and Safety, Environmental Compliance, and so on.

Individuals in operating and staff functions (such as Finance) will from time to time identify risks to the organization and it is critical that they be heard. While the establishment of a whistleblower line can help, it is far more effective if the culture of the organization enables these people to speak up and be heard without fear of retaliation.

10. Does compliance 'chase the bus', or is it part of strategy-setting and initiative decisions?

In many organizations, managing compliance is an afterthought. The decision is made to expand into a new country or deliver a new product or service, without serious consideration of the potential implications of ensuring the organization is at all times compliant with applicable laws and regulations. Compliance personnel may, at best, be informed of the decision so they can initiate efforts to ensure compliance. At worst, they find out late and have to "chase the bus" to try and catch up and get on board.

Ideally, compliance requirements, risks, and related costs and opportunities are considered when strategies are established and related projects and initiatives planned and executed.

Compliance personnel, extending to managers in functions such as information security and tax, should be brought into planning for new initiatives early. This not only provides valuable information for the owners of the initiatives to consider when assessing costs, risks, and potential benefits, but enables actions to be taken to limit potential exposures from non-compliance.

One question that can be useful is for the owners of an initiative to ask "who might be affected should we go ahead with this initiative" and bring them into the discussion.

As with so many of these issues, a healthy corporate culture that encourages sharing and openness is more likely to ensure that everybody who can contribute to the success of new initiatives, including compliance personnel, are included in early planning.

11. Does the board receive timely, quality, reliable, current, and useful information to advise on strategy, monitor executive performance, and function effectively?

Survey after survey, including "Bridging Board Gaps" (at www.directorscenter.com), have identified the flow of timely, complete, and useful information to the board as one of the greatest challenges to effective governance. Richard Beattie, in that report, is quoted as saying "Boards only know what the CEO and CFO tell them. Nothing more. This is a significant problem." Olivia Kirtley commented that "Information is the lifeblood of effective governance."

Striking to the heart of the problem is this quote from *Bridging Board Gaps*:

> "Many governance problems have arisen from poor management decisions, hidden and often compounded through inadequate information disclosure to the board..... However, if the board relies solely on management reports, the risk is that information may be incomplete, filtered, or edited, even in good-faith ways."

Best practice is for transparency and trust between the board and executive management. Management does not hold anything back, nor wait for perfect information to inform the board. The board has established and management understands expectations for what should be provided to the directors, when, and how.

In the question, I included a number of adjectives to describe the information that the board should receive if it is to effectively advise on strategy and monitor performance:

Timely – is the information provided to the board promptly? This is especially important when events escalate quickly and timely responses are vital

Quality – does the board receive sufficient, relevant information?

Reliable – is the information complete, accurate, and unvarnished?

Current – is the information up-to-date?

Useful – is the information in a form that is clear and easy to use? Does it enable the directors to understand not only the symptoms but the causes of any issue? Are they able to get information in sufficient detail, and is the information delivered to them where they need it (e.g., using mobile technology)?

Unfortunately, the surveys that report board dissatisfaction with the quality and completeness of the information they receive don't explain why the directors are not demanding change. Boards should remember that management reports to them and demand change, setting expectations of what they will receive, when, and in what form.

12. Does the board have continuing assurance of the above?

The board is reliant on management's processes for providing necessary information to establish appropriate strategies, execute on those strategies and deliver performance, consider and manage risk, and remain in compliance.

The external auditors provide a level of assurance to the board that management's financial statements can be relied upon, but (with a few exceptions) they don't provide opinions on management's other processes. For those, the board has to rely on the internal audit function and other assurance groups (which may include a risk office; environmental, health and safety function, etc.)

In most countries, the board (or its audit committee) is expected to ensure that the organization has effective risk management and internal control processes. Those should extend to include the processes the board relies on to provide effective governance and oversight.

In my opinion, the board (or its committees) should ensure that they have a reasonable basis for any assessment they may make on the adequacy of risk management and internal control – and the best source for that assurance is the internal audit function.

I believe that internal audit should provide an annual report that includes a formal opinion on governance, risk management, and related internal control processes. That opinion will be based on the work they have performed, which will typically focus on the more significant risks to the enterprise as a whole.

Why does it make sense to discuss GRC?

I am on record as saying that it only makes sense to discuss GRC if:

1. Everyone is using the term in the same way, and
2. The discussion is about what I and OCEG refer to as GRC (i.e., the need for all the various parts of the organization, from the board through executive management and including how the organization addresses performance, risk, and compliance) to work together, in harmony

The problem when talking about GRC is that sometimes it takes focus away from the serious issues that most organizations have in the individual areas of risk management, governance, compliance, performance management, strategy management, and so on.

While it is true that it is often necessary for one area to compromise so that all can function better together, most organizations still have a long way to go before the components within GRC are even close to effective.

For example, most organizations have not progressed beyond periodic review and discussion of a point-in-time list of so-called top risks. They have a lot of work to do, embedding the consideration of risk into daily decision-making, before they should expend a lot of energy integrating, say, risk and financial forecasting or planning.

Let me close this document by recommending that every organization ensure that it understands all its internal obstacles to success. That will include:

- Immature processes for risk management, performance management, the provision of information to decision-makers, compliance management, and so on
- Ineffective coordination among and between the various components of GRC as they work in silos

The executive management team should recognize that these are obstacles that make it far more difficult for them to achieve the potential of the organization. They should prioritize projects, with assigned owners from the executive management team, to address them.

This project to address shortcomings in and between the various components of GRC is what I would call a GRC project.

[i] By way of full disclosure, OCEG has made me a Fellow in recognition of my GRC thought leadership. However, the content of this paper and the opinions I express are not influenced by them.

[ii] OCEG (see www.oceg.org) describes itself as "a nonprofit organization that uniquely helps organizations drive **Principled Performance®** by enhancing corporate culture and integrating governance, risk management, and compliance processes by providing:

- Guidelines and Standards
- Community of Practice
- Evaluation Criteria and Benchmarks.

"**Principled Performance®** is the reliable achievement of objectives while addressing uncertainty and acting with integrity."

www.ingramcontent.com/pod-product-compliance
Lightning Source LLC
Chambersburg PA
CBHW071554170526
45166CB00004B/1661